Also by Micah Johns:

Gideon
John Walker and the Forbidden Fire

Also by Christianna Johns:

God and Fireflies

ISAAC
AND
REBEKAH

An epic poem by Micah and Christianna Johns

The Tale of Isaac
(by Micah Johns):
Begun June 1, 2005;
Finished May 7, 2016.

The Song of Rebekah
(by Christianna Johns):
Begun January 13, 2021;
Finished January 14, 2021.

Cover art by Micah Johns.

Dedicated to

Christianna R.M. Johns,

the love of my life.

—Micah

Contents:

Based on the true story

as found in the book of Genesis,

chapter twenty-four,

the first book of the Holy Scriptures.

ISAAC
AND
REBEKAH

Part One:

The Tale of

Isaac

I: The Man

Across the seas in arid land,
Beyond demand for billowing sail
Roused by a roaring, rushing gale,
And far from need for anchor's mass
Heaved upward by a hefty hand;

Away from talk of aft and fore,
Mention of oar, of mighty craft,
Where worthless is the wooden raft,
And where no fleets of armies pass,
Swept by the surging sea to war;

Near jagged peaks of naked stone
Out in the lonely, open hills,
Where on the wind the warbled trills
Of bright-eyed birds are often heard—
Loud, lively tunes of lovely tone—

Down in these hills there dwelt of old
A tall, broad-shouldered, aging man,
Now thirty-nine, of noble clan.
Dark were his eyes, which deeply stirred
When wished he for a wife to hold;

Entangled locks grew endlessly,
Like roots of trees, below his face.
Long were his limbs: His legs could race
As fast as those of anyone
Designed for dashing desperately;

Vitality- and vigor-filled,
Agile and skilled, his arms and hands
No equal knew in native lands:
Commendably his chores were done
Ere evening, as he ever willed.

Dense robes with grime and dirt and dust
In spots encrusted—in no way
Neat or like new—both night and day
Yet shrouded his once youthful frame,
Each easily having earned his trust.

And his thick mane of auburn hair
Raged like a flare when radiant light
Shone sharply from the sun: As bright
As fire it fell, fierce as a flame—
Neck-length now, and in need of care.

II: Loneliness and Desire

Down in a deep ravine one night,
This weary man walked briskly through
Harsh undergrowth. The half-moon's light
Exposed the earth o'er which he flew—
Long, lonely paths he hardly knew.

Out on his own, by no one seen;
Restless and ragged, far from home;
Dreaming of dancing with a queen,
Hungry for romance, he did roam,
An aching soul away from home.

Desire to drink the draughts of love,
Born in him when he was a boy;
Longing to hold a lady of
Enchantment, ere all hope of joy
Stole off, now seized this grown-up boy.

Since childhood he had stood apart,
Expressing not his emptiness.
Distractions cured his desolate heart,
His hopes forgotten, wounds to dress
Ignored, wrapped in feigned happiness.

Many a maiden he had seen,
Intrigued by their inviting eyes.
None, though, were pure; not one was clean—
Each pleasantly ensnared by lies,
Vainly evading searching eyes.

Early these erring girls he had
Rejected, and their reckless ways.
Years later, yet immensely glad
Was he that weakness in those days
And lust had not advised his ways.

Yet now, his youth a memory,
He wondered whether hope remained.
Each night seemed an eternity—
Stone-cold, as empty silence reigned
And all alone this man remained.

Impatient with integrity,
Darkened by doubts, he entertained
The thought that his priority
Of seeking one by lies unstained
Truly had crushed the hope it feigned.

III: Yahweh's Faithfulness

He skirted now a softly singing stream,
Eyes dimmed by roiling clouds which veiled the light
Cascading from the stars, the moon's dull gleam
Half-hidden as it circled o'er the night.
Imagining his mother's twinkling eyes,
Envisioning his father at her side,
Feared he that all their promises were lies.
"Someday," they'd said, "we'll find for you a bride.
Expectantly await her; cheerfully
Rejoice, for Yahweh surely will provide!
Vast as the starry fields your clan shall be;
All through the earth your family will reside.
No idle words are these, for from Yahweh
They came, who will fulfill them all someday."

If all these words were true, then why was there
No maiden at his side this lonely night?
He wondered, as he fell down in despair,
If Yahweh even cared about his plight.
So many times throughout the passing years
His mother had the wondrous tale retold
Of how Yahweh had seen the bitter tears
Upon her face and shown her kindness. Old
She was and, having never given birth,
Expected all her days to end in grief.
He promised her a son, and, filled with mirth,
One son she bore, despite her disbelief.
Learned she to trust in Yahweh's faithfulness;
Dark doubts her promised son did now express.

The moonlight nearly vanished from the sky,
He noticed now a gentle rain the land
Enveloping with mist both far and nigh.
On shaky feet he forced himself to stand,
Now hastening into the hills once more.
Ere long, he saw a darkly looming hill
Imprinted in his mind from years before.
Nightmares that dreadful mountain gave him still.
Carefree and young, a sudden journey he
Had taken with his father. When the place
At last they reached where they that hill could see,
Red shone the sun upon its distant face.
Glorious and grim Moriah did appear,
Evoking thoughts of both wonder and fear.

Onward they trod through thickly tangled brush.
Far to the west clouds dark as night did form;
All round the mountain fell an eerie hush,
Like silence just before a violent storm.
Long thought he of the sacrifice that they
That day would make, as Yahweh did require.
His father bore a knife, the beast to slay,
And flint to start the fiercely blazing fire;
The firewood the child carried. Yet
He wondered why no lamb was at their side.
Explained his father that they must not fret:
"Have faith, my son, for Yahweh will provide."
And soon the place upon Moriah they
Did reach where they the animal would slay.

Peered round the boy intently for a sheep
Under the trees and in the thickets near
This glade of broken stones and grasses deep.
Yet any sign he did not see or hear
Of animals. Meanwhile,.his father wrought
Upon the site an altar with great skill.
Ready it was, and still the child naught
Had found which spoke of lambs upon the hill.
At dusk, they piled the wood, which he had cast
Nearby, upon the altar. Suddenly
Deranged, it seemed, his father bound him fast.
"Untie me!" cried he, desperate to be free.
No mercy showed his father, tying him
Down to the altar limb by struggling limb.

Eyes wide, he watched his father's silhouette
Reach down and draw the brightly gleaming knife.
"My father, no!" he cried, and prayed that yet
Yahweh might see his plight and save his life.
The blade above his heart, he knew that he
Had to his death been utterly betrayed.
"I'm sorry," said his father quietly.
Grim-faced, he swiftly downward plunged the blade.
"Hurt not the boy!" a voice called suddenly.
"I know you fear me now, for you have not
Withheld your son, your only son, from me.
A clan too great to count shall be your lot.
Now free the boy, my servant Abraham,
That he might live, and slay instead the ram."

Yahweh thus spoke. And lo! their eyes caught sight
Of a ram in a nearby thicket. They
Upon the altar in the faint moonlight
Then sacrificed that beast without delay.
Once more his faithfulness Yahweh had shown.
Soaked presently with rain, his tent now near;
Wayworn and weary, restless and alone;
Entranced no more, he shed a single tear.
Although his heart was filled with hope once more,
Relentless doubts still lingered in his mind.
Believed he what had happened years before,
Yet wondered whether he would ever find
The maiden pure for whom his heart did leap.
He entered then his tent and went to sleep.

IV: Season of Waiting

Empty morns and evenings passed,
Long loveless days and lonely nights.
Often, he, with aching heart,
Roamed round along the rocky heights.

Daylight waned and darkness grew;
Thick, thundering clouds poured thrashing rains;
Hillsides, lashed by howling winds,
Echoed back their eerie strains.

Glumly autumn's gloom was spread
O'er all the land by ancient hands;
Dawn came dim and dusk too quick,
Ordered thus by old commands.

Far abroad he fared those days,
Hunting beasts in hollows deep;
Each animal this archer shot
An arrow laid to endless sleep.

Vales and mountains vast he crossed,
Eager streams and empty plains.
Near his dwelling now, he labored
All day in the autumn rains.

Now arrived the night on which
Death his mother dear had slain
Two years past; he tensely cried
His heart's lament, a haunting strain.

Ever darker each day grew,
Gold now turning grey and bleak.
Ominously, icy gales
Drove in with a dreadful shriek.

Onward winter's onslaught came,
Filling him with fear once more.
Each night he lay all alone
As on the endless hours wore.

Rueful and bereft of joy,
Torn he was between his lustful
Hunger and his hope in Yahweh's
Troth; Yahweh he chose to trust.

His heart grew even heavier
As Eli left one early morn,
Travelling far on trails which many
Years had seen, paths used and worn.

Of all their servants honored most,
Unto them was Eli loyal,
Warden good and wise of all
In Abraham's house and on his soil.

Lonely though Isaac lay at night,
Longing for a loving wife,
Now the winter's night gave way
Once again to warmth and life.

V: The Maiden

Then one day, sunlight on the trees
Gleaming, leaves rustling in the breeze,
Ere twilight's gloom devoured the day
This man set out to think and pray.

As down the greying hill he strode
Where with his father he abode,
It came into his mind that he
Forever quite alone might be.

Eyes darkened, the sun's final rays
Fast fading into twilight's haze,
Out of his mind this thought he sent,
Resolved that he should be content.

Mind resting in the promise of
Yahweh's unfailing, faithful love,
Slowly, head down, his way he made
Onto a field shrouded in shade.

Now looking up, this ruddy man
Far off descried a caravan,
Revealed beneath the blue-grey sky,
Of men and camels drawing nigh.

Moving towards them, perceived he then
That he beheld his father's men;
Heart leaping, he rejoiced to see
Eli among this company.

Drawing near, though, among these men
A maiden's form he noticed. When
Upon her partly veiled face
Gazed he, his heart began to race.

Hope, like a spring, within him welled
That she whom now his eyes beheld,
Enraptured, had her former life
Renounced and come to be his wife.

So running to the servant's side
On flying feet, he loudly cried,
"Friend, welcome back! Glad is my heart
That we no longer are apart!"

He whispered then, "But who is she,
Eli, that moves so gracefully,
Covered in black, among your crew?
And why has she come here with you?"

"Not till we reach our tents," Eli
Answered, "shall you the reason why
A maiden walks among us learn.
Now let us to our home return!"

In haste they headed towards the hill
That housed their tents, where in the chill
Eli this tale by firelight
Shared with his master's son that night:

VI: The Servant's Story

A long while back, ere winter's gloom had passed,
Mindful of his son's visage, pale and grim,
One morning Abraham summoned at last
None other than Eli and said to him,
"Go now, my servant, to the distant land
Whence long ago we travelled far and wide,
Here to find rest once more, led by the hand
Of Yahweh, who has ever been our guide.
Make me a promise by Yahweh that there,
In his direction trusting, you will find
Among my relatives a gracious, fair
Maiden of noble heart. Then far behind
Leave that country and bring her here, that she
In marriage joined to Isaac might then be."

"Very well," Eli said. "But what if she
Insists on staying there? If so, I am
Not sure how best to serve your son. Should he
Go back there with me?" "No," said Abraham.
"By Yahweh swear, who rules the earth, and who
Upon heaven's throne sits in majesty,
That never to that far-off country you
Will take my son. For Yahweh said to me,
'I to your offspring Canaan's land will give.
Leave your homeland behind, and follow my
Lead to the place wherein your clan shall live.
Go, and do not look back, for your steps I
O'er vale and mountain will to Canaan guide,
The land where your descendants shall reside.'"

Obediently this oath Eli then swore:
"My lord, I'll never to that country take
Your son—lest I be cursed forevermore!
Cursed may I be if I this promise break!"
On that same morning, he, without delay,
Undaunted by the task that lay ahead,
Not troubled by the cold, which would give way
To warmth when spring arrived in winter's stead,
Readied himself and summoned to his side
Young fellow servants stout of heart and limb,
Assistance on his journey to provide.
Nigh they ten camels guided unto him—
Dependable, strong beasts, on which these men
Many fine, costly items loaded then.

"Your servants," to his lord, as he drew nigh
Once more to him ere leaving, Eli said,
"Will at your word bid this fair land goodbye.
Now shall we go?" With that, he bowed his head.
"Remain here no more," Abraham replied.
"Each one of you, with Yahweh's blessing, go."
Lifting his head, "My lord," Eli then cried,
"A greater master I shall never know
Than you—save him who is the Lord of all.
I will to you be faithful: Having crossed
Vast hills and plains, vales deep and mountains tall—
Even if I endangered am or lost—
Still I shall serve you. I will not rebel
Against you!" Then those two men said, "Farewell!"

Now free to leave, Eli without delay
Departed, over hills and mountains vast
Guiding his comrades northeastward, the way
Etched clearly in his mind from journeys past.
The sky was iron grey, shrouded in gloom;
A frigid wind swept through the open hills.
"We should turn back!" one servant yelled. "Our doom
Is nigh! Before this dreadful weather kills
First one, then all of us, we should retreat!"
Eli laughed heartily and said, "My friend,
Foul weather on this journey we shall meet;
One thing we shall not meet, though, is our end.
Relax, and brave this bitter cold with me,
My friend; for warm you once again shall be."

"Your words," the other servant answered him,
"Sound hollow to my ears." And yet he spoke
Of doom no more and uttered omens grim
No longer, but, wrapped tightly in his cloak,
Instead continued on without complaint.
So none, despite the bitter cold, turned back.
All day they travelled, till the sunlight, faint
And grey, dissolved, the heavens now pitch-black.
Camp then they quickly set up for the night,
Tying the camels to a stand of oaks.
Hungry, they ate a meal by firelight,
Exchanging wild tales and sharing jokes.
Sleep then they sought, each lying on his side,
Exhausted, as the fire slowly died.

Refreshed, at dawn they rose and their campsite
Vacated, once again making their way
Across the wind-swept country, morning's light
Now gleaming faintly through clouds thick and grey.
They journeyed on for several weeks, past plains
And mountains and through rivers swift and cold,
Soaked often by the driving winter rains,
Kept constantly on course by Eli's old,
Enduring knowledge of those rugged lands.
Day after day he led them faithfully,
His fellow servants keeping his commands.
Inspired those men were by his loyalty,
Matchless and fierce, to Abraham, their lord,
Whom all of them now served in one accord.

Harsh winter soon gave way to mild spring:
A fragrant scent came wafting on the breeze;
The sky turned blue, the grey clouds scattering;
Intricate songs up in the flowering trees
Flight-weary birds sang cheerfully; between
The budding boughs fell shafts of sunlight gold;
Hard, faded earth, now thawed, grew soft and green:
Ended was winter's nighttime, stark and cold.
With vigor fresh, their waning strength renewed,
Onward the servants travelled day by day,
Marching through foreign regions, till they viewed
Afar through morning's mist, hazy and grey,
Nahor at last with squinting eyes—the town
In which their master's kin had settled down.

Swiftly along that final stretch they walked
Under clear skies. Both Eli and his men
Nearer for hours slowly drew, eyes locked,
Wide with excitement, on the village. Then,
Intent on reaching Nahor by nightfall,
Lest yet another day it take them their
Long, tiring journey to complete, they all
Increased their pace. And so, exhausted, ere
Nighttime arrived, while yet the westward sun
Glowed gold and scarlet, just outside the town
They came across a well and, one by one,
Onto the ground without a word fell down:
Completely worn out by their arduous quest,
One final time the servants stopped to rest.

Mere moments later, Eli stood once more,
Exhorting all the others from the dust
Beneath them to arise as well. "Before
Attending to ourselves," he said, "we must
Care for our camels' needs, that they might first
Kneel down to rest beside this well. Though we
Without a doubt are hungry, and our thirst
Is very great indeed, we ought to see
To their needs first." So, rising quickly, they
Hastened to aid each camel strong and stout.
Moved suddenly to prayer, without delay
Eli himself knelt down. And blocking out
The noise and movement coming from the crowd
Of men surrounding him, he cried aloud:

"Today I seek your favor, O Yahweh;
Hear my request from where you dwell on high.
If you are willing, even while I pray,
See fit to make our quest successful. I
Learned long ago that you are great in power,
And that nothing's too difficult for you.
Now, Lord of Abraham, this very hour,
Deal kindly with my master—as you do
Steadfastly with all those who fear your name.
Help me to carry out the daunting task
Assigned to me; in failure and shame
Let us not leave this land. Again I ask:
Lend us your aid, according to our need,
In order that our efforts might succeed!"

Then, looking towards the town and coming to
His feet, excitement showing in his eyes,
Eli continued praying: "Lord, may you
Not fail to hear your humble servant's cries
Today! Behold, I stand beside this spring
As the young women of the town draw nigh,
Keen to return to Nahor carrying,
Ere darkness falls, jars full of water. By
Your goodness, may it come to pass that when
One of these maidens for a drink I ask
Upon our timely meeting, and she then
Responds, 'I'll go beyond that simple task:
Some water for your camels, too, I'll heave
Out of this well, my lord, before I leave'—

"Noble and pure in every way, may she
Be—at long last—the one whom you have set
Apart your servant Isaac's wife to be.
Creator of all things, do not forget
Kindness, by granting my request, to show
To Abraham, my master." Silence fell
Once more as Eli finished praying, though
The now-approaching maidens broke its spell:
Heedless of Eli and his weary crew,
Each girl strode directly to the well;
Conversing loudly, water now they drew,
One at a time. And soon Eli could tell,
Unsettled by their speech, that of this lot
Not one would be the maiden whom he sought.

The line grew quickly shorter as the sun
Retreated towards the earth. But Eli knew
Yahweh would surely, ere the day was done,
Yet bring to him the noble maiden, true
Of heart, for whom he searched. Repelled by the
Unruly talk of those who from the well
Continued to draw clear, clean water, he
Away from them now turned. His gaze thus fell,
Most unexpectedly, upon the bright,
Enchanting face of one who stood apart
From all the other girls, clearly quite
Repulsed by their vile speech. Now Eli's heart,
Old though it was, was pounding; for he thought
Maybe he'd finally found the one he sought!

Motionless, Eli watched expectantly
As calmly the lone maiden, radiant and
Kind-eyed, stepped forth and took her place at the
End of the line. A minute later, stand
She did, alone, before the spring, her jar
Upheld by strong and steady hands. And now,
Ready at last, the jar she lowered far
Enough into the deep shaft to allow
The needed water to be scooped out. Then,
Heaving with all her might, she pulled it out
And lifted it onto her shoulder. When
The jar was set in place, she turned about,
Yet one more time the tough task to begin
Of hauling water homeward for her kin.

Up from the well the maiden strode without
Delay. But Eli hesitated, full
Of sudden, overwhelming fear and doubt.
Notions and visions dark and terrible
Of certain failure rose within his mind.
Though he had planned a moment earlier
To hurry towards the girl and, with a kind
And cheerful word of greeting, speak to her,
Kept now he was from acting by these grim,
Enthralling thoughts as round his mind they swirled.
Mad his entire mission seemed to him!
Yet these immobilizing thoughts he hurled
Swiftly aside, by his desire to
Obey his master filled with faith anew.

No longer bound by fear and doubt, Eli
Boldly and quickly towards the maiden marched
At once. And as unto her he drew nigh,
Cried he, "Fair maiden, wait! My mouth is parched.
Know not I do how far or for how long
Today my weary feet have travelled." She
Halted and turned around as, loud and strong,
Eli continued: "Please, that I might be
Refreshed, give me some water from your jar."
Eyeing him with compassion, she replied,
"A stranger to your servant though you are,
By me shall your request not be denied:
Refreshment, that your strength might be restored
Again, find in this water now, my lord."

Her jar she quickly lowered to her hands,
And he, thanking the maiden, drank his fill.
"My hands shall now do what my heart commands,"
She told him then: "Your camels' needs they will
Attend to." The remaining water she
Into a nearby empty trough poured out.
Drawing from the deep shaft repeatedly,
The trough she swiftly filled. Without a doubt
Her heart, Eli observed, was true, as though
Engraved with kindness and humility.
Leading the camels to the trough, the glow
Of sunset lighting up his features, he
Reflected on the deeds the girl had done—
Deeds fitting for the wife of his lord's son.

Then, as with all her might the maiden drew

Her jar one final time out of the spring,

Eli quickly and quietly pulled two

Gold bracelets and a matching gold nose ring

Out of one of the many sacks whose rough,

Dust-covered cords had stayed tied since the day

On which the journey, strenuous and tough,

From Abraham's abode, so far away,

Had started. With that jewelry in hand,

Eli drew near the girl once more. And he

Asked her, "Whose daughter are you, gracious and

Virtuous maiden?" For a moment, she

Examined the man's eyes; she must have spied

No cause for fear therein, for she replied:

"What you desire to know, your ears shall hear.

Hearken unto my speech: I am the child

Of Bethuel, the son of Nahor's dear,

Beloved wife." At this, the servant smiled,

Rejoicing in his spirit that the son

Of Nahor was her father. "Is there space

Under your father's roof for everyone

Gathered here?" he inquired of her. "No place

Have we to spend the night." These kind words then

The maiden offered: "There is room inside

My father's house for you and all your men;

Each one of you tonight shall there abide.

Our guests your camels too, my lord, shall be

Until the light of dawn once more we see."

Then said the servant, "Thank you for your kind
Offer; I shall accept it gratefully.
First, though, to know your name I am inclined.
My name is Eli. What is yours?" And she
Yielded to his request: "Rebekah. My
Father and mother gave that name to me;
And by that name I still am called." Eli
Then held before her eyes the jewelry
He'd taken from the sack. And, with delight,
Explained he, "These as gifts for you were meant,
Rebekah. They are treasures, fair and bright,
Sent by my master for me to present,
Here at my lengthy journey's end, unto
One worthy girl. That worthy one is you!"

Uncertainly she smiled and shook her head.
"Sir, you and I are strangers. How can these
Extraordinary words be true?" she said.
He answered, "Yahweh, whom I aim to please,
On this long quest has acted as our guide,
Leading us towards your town, then to this well
Directing us, where my keen eyes descried,
At last, one noble maiden. I shall tell
No more of this to you till we reach your
Dwelling. Put down your jar now, and I'll place
My master's gifts upon you; for before
You go, your arms and nose they ought to grace."
Nodding, she set the jar down; and his hands
Adorned her bare wrists with the twin gold bands.

Then, though the maiden made no movement, she
Instinctively in shock and anguish screamed,
Voicing her pain as, full of sympathy,
Eli her nose pierced with the ring, which gleamed
Like fire flaring from her nostrils, whence
A stream of glistening blood, like molten ore,
Now flowed. Rebekah—trembling, pale, and tense—
Dropped to her knees. Her cry had lasted for
A moment only, but the pain was by
No means subsiding. So the servant bent
Down next to her and, handing her a dry
White cloth with which the blood to soak up, lent
His hand to her for comfort, which she grabbed
Outright as with the cloth her face she dabbed.

Standing nearby in silence, Eli's crew
Patiently waited, tired and worn, yet stout
Of heart. After a while, Eli, who
Knelt yet beside Rebekah, looked about:
Eastward, the sky grew dark as twilight fell;
Thick shadows, as the sun sank westward, crept
Over the landscape rapidly, the well
Masking in gloom. The servant's bright gaze swept,
Ere long, back to the girl: Her face conveyed
A sense of calm and peace; fresh purpose and
New fortitude her sparkling eyes displayed.
Determinedly did she release his hand,
Proceed to rise to her full height, and say,
"Rare treasures you bestowed on me today.

"Once home, unto your master please convey
My gratitude! His generosity
Is undeserved." "On the glad, joyous day,"
Said Eli, "when my lord once more I see,
Express your thanks to him I shall." Then he,
Down on his knees already, bowed his head
Meekly and said, "Praise be to Yahweh, the
Eternal Lord! His servant he has led
On the right path and granted him success;
No obstacles have kept me from the kin
Of Abraham. His constant faithfulness
And kindness to my master—proven in
The past—Yahweh has not abandoned; to
His word he once again has proven true!"

Silence now, as the servant stilled his tongue
And unashamedly bowed low before
Yahweh in praise and adoration, hung
In the cool air. Though on the evening wore,
Nobody made a sound. But when Eli
Got up at last, Rebekah spoke once more:
"The hour grows late! To my home quickly I
Ought to return, there to prepare for your
Yet unannounced arrival! I shall bid
One of my kin to come and guide you hence;
Until he does, wait here." That said, she did
Run towards the town in haste. "This day's events,"
One of the servants then remarked, "shall be
Forever etched upon my memory.

"For here I've witnessed wondrous things. Yahweh
Surely has, in response to Eli's prayer,
Performed amazing deeds. What can I say?
Reverence for Yahweh overwhelms me! There
Is no one like him!" Someone else agreed:
"No one, indeed, is like him! None of these
Great things by fate or fortune were decreed;
In answer to his servant Eli's pleas
Were they decreed by Yahweh!" Others then
In praise of Yahweh spoke. When they at last
Lapsed into silence, still that crowd of men
Lingered there with their camels while the vast
Grey skies began to glow with faint starlight.
In minutes, dusk had faded into night.

Voice raised in horror, suddenly Eli
Exclaimed, "I have been heartless! Here you stand,
Thirsty and parched as dust, my friends, while I
Have had my fill of water, like a land
In which plants flourish! Bear with me; your need
Shall soon be met." His own jar swiftly he
Lowered into the well; and, with great speed
And strength, he filled it. His whole company
Now quenched their thirst. They, at Eli's command,
Did not disturb Rebekah's jar, which she
Had left, yet full of water, close at hand;
Eli's alone they drank from. Finally, he,
When they had finished, heard one servant cry,
"I hear the sound of someone drawing nigh!"

"Look! Over there!" another called. The soft
Light of the newly risen quarter-moon
Shining down dimly from its eastward loft,
Eli could see a man approaching. Soon,
No hesitation in his stride, the man
Drew close. And, halting near the servant's crew,
He said, "Hello! Of Nahor's noble clan
I am a member. I was sent here to
Show you to our abode." Peering round, then
Asked he, "Which one of you is named Eli?"
Now, stepping forth, the leader of the men
Gathered there answered, "I am thus named." "Why,
Eli," the man laughed merrily, "are you all
Lingering at this well after nightfall?

"Because," without the least delay the man
Explained, "—lest all night long this land you roam—
For me you wait, to lead your caravan
Of men and camels to my father's home.
Rest there you soon shall find, my friend! You are
Expected by my father—you, who by
Yahweh are blessed. So come! From here, not far
Our destination is." Then did he cry,
"Unknown to you my name is yet! Friend, you
Should know who'll guide your steps. Laban, the son
Of Bethuel, am I. Now let us to
The house of my kin hasten, everyone!
Have I not made it ready? Quick! Prepare
At once to leave, and I will take you there!"

Thus Eli, eyes aglow, responded: "To
Your dwelling, Laban, we shall soon make haste!
Once we are ready, we will follow you
Unswervingly. No moment shall we waste!"
Called he then to his men, "Let us be off
At once!" According to this brisk command,
No time they lost in heading to the trough,
Guiding the animals towards Laban, and
Embarking with him on the road that would
Take them to the abode of Bethuel.
After a while, outside that house they stood,
Where the girl's full jar, which, left near the well
In haste, had now been borne back to the town
For her, Eli's stiff, aching arms set down.

Efficiently his comrades at his word,
Fresh vigor in their limbs, their cargo pulled
Off of the camels, offering that herd
Relief. The household servants Laban told,
Meanwhile, to treat their guests as his own kin.
"You must," he ordered, "make them welcome, for
Servants they are of Nahor's brother." In
Obedience, they labored at that chore:
No small amount of straw and fodder they
Fetched for the camels; that the travellers might
Rinse off the dirt and dust which day by day
On their sore feet had settled, into sight
Mirror-like water, clear and clean, as well
The servants brought whose lord was Bethuel.

"Hello!" a deep-voiced man soon cried as he,
Exiting the abode, appeared. "I am
Rebekah's father. One of you must be
Eli, the chief servant of Abraham."
"I am the one," said Eli, "whom you've named."
"Friend, surely you and your companions in
This house of mine shall be," the man proclaimed,
"Honored. For herein dwell your master's kin.
Eli," the man continued, "you converse
With him whose name is Bethuel, the son
Of Nahor. Here, your name no one shall curse,
My friend! Now one last thing, and I'll be done:
A feast with all of you we now will share:
Naught in its preparation did we spare!"

Into the dwelling then his guests he led.
Sweet, rich aromas filled the air. A plate,
Upon which choice, delicious food was spread,
Now a man placed in front of Eli. "Wait!
Will I now eat?" said Eli. "No—not till
I've said all that I have to say." The man
Lifted the plate once more; the room went still.
Laban said, "Speak your mind." Eli began
Informing of his mission, then, his hosts:
"Nahor's sojourning brother, Abraham,
Great riches has acquired (of which he boasts
To none). A witness I, his servant, am
Of how Yahweh, the mighty Master he
Chooses to serve, has blessed him lavishly.

"Old though she was, Sarah, my master's bride,
Many years back bore him a single son.
Each thing he now owns will, once he has died,
Belong to Isaac, Sarah's child—his one
And only heir. My lord a solemn vow
Commanded me to make—a vow that I
Knew I must keep: that I in loyalty now
Would carry out a great assignment. My
Instructions were to leave at once and come
To the land where his father's family lives;
Having done so, then, with assistance from
Yahweh, to find among his relatives
One maiden who, in marriage with his son
Uniting, would become with Isaac one."

Then his whole tale Eli recounted to
His listeners. He told them how he then
Enlisted several helpers; how this crew
Nigh unto him brought camels; how these men—
Young, strong, and faithful—piled on the backs
Of those ten camels bags of costly goods
Until the moment when all of those sacks
Were finally loaded; and how, cloaks and hoods
In place to insulate them from the cold,
Left they with him in haste. He spoke of their
Long journey: how on pathways worn and old
Bravely they walked, not yielding to despair
Even though trials they faced, nor quitting when
Returning home seemed best to those good men.

Excitedly did he narrate the last
Leg of their trip, relating how they came—
Exhausted from their travels, yet steadfast
And sure—to the spring earlier that same
Soul-stirring day. His faith in Yahweh he
Expressed to those who, thrilled by what they heard,
Did hearken to his voice: His fervent plea
For Yahweh's help he, nearly word for word,
Repeated boldly. He went on to tell
Of his encounter with the girl: how he
Met and spoke with Rebekah at the well
That evening; and how, filled with kindness, she
Humbly served him, thereby revealing her
Incredibly outstanding character.

Spoke then the servant animatedly
Of his conviction that this maiden fair
And noble was the one who soon would be
The wife of his lord's one and only heir.
He talked about the bracelets and the ring
Of gold which he adorned her with. And he,
Finally his epic story finishing,
Made known his praise of Yahweh now to the
Intently focused crowd, whose ears desired
None of his words to miss: He told how he,
Elated at the way things had transpired,
Offered praise unto Yahweh, faithfully
Naming him as the one who'd led him to
Laban's sister, kind-hearted, fair, and true.

"You've now," Eli concluded, "heard my tale.
Decide you must, my lords, Rebekah's fate.
Ought she to join me on my homeward trail?
Now take some time my words to contemplate
Once and for all, Laban and Bethuel.
Then tell me if kindness and faithfulness
To Abraham you'll show. Must Isaac dwell
Alone, or will you grant my quest success?"
Keen eyes throughout the room now shifted from
Eli to Bethuel and Laban, though
Many of them glanced back and forth, and some
Yet lingered on the servant. Voices low,
Spoke then the two lords of that house with each
Other as they considered Eli's speech.

"No words we utter," Bethuel, once his
Brief conversation with his son was through,
Announced, "can change the outcome. Laban is
Convinced, and so am I, that Yahweh, who
Kindness and faithfulness has surely shown
To Nahor's brother, orchestrated in
His goodness these amazing things." "Unknown
Ere your arrival, Eli, to her kin
Rebekah's fate was," Laban added. "These
Events have made it clear, though. And we will
Submit to Yahweh's will. For his decrees,
Once issued, who can alter? To fulfill
The wishes of your master we indeed
Have humbly and wholeheartedly agreed."

Eyes full of raw emotion, Nahor's son
Summoned the maiden to his side. Then, to
Eli he said, "My friend, your quest is done!
Rebekah shall go with you when your crew
Vacates my dwelling, that she might become,
As Yahweh has directed, Isaac's bride.
Now let us feast!" And so, eyes turning from
The three who'd spoken, and mouths opening wide,
Partook the folk of Nahor of the meal.
Uneaten, though, for quite some time remained
The servant's food. Unable to conceal
His awe of him who o'er the whole world reigned
In splendor, Eli, heedless of the crowd
Surrounding him, before that great King bowed.

He rose and called his men then, and, their food
Abandoning, they followed him outside.
Numerous treasures gold- and silver-hued,
Designed with care and wrought with skill and pride;
Unique and costly gems, the likes of which
None of those servants owned; fine garments by
Deft fingers woven, beautiful and rich—
Eli, with his lord's wishes to comply,
Retrieved, with the assistance of his men,
These precious items from the sacks which they
Had brought with them on their long trip. They then,
Entering the abode without delay,
Those goods in hand, to where the girl beside
Her father sat did with one purpose stride.

"I'm honored to present you with these fine
Gifts from my master," Eli said, once they
Had halted, to Rebekah. "As a sign
Of my lord's favor, I a rich array,
Fair maiden, of good things now give to you."
He lavished on her, then, the best of the
Items sent by his lord. To Laban, who
Stood near his sister, watching eagerly,
Many luxurious gifts he gave as well.
And at the feet of the girl's mother, who
Sat, weeping softly, next to Bethuel,
Treasures he laid down in abundance. To
Eli, though, said the maiden's father, "No
Riches or goods on me shall you bestow.

"As costly as these things are, I shall still
Be sundered from my daughter; nothing can
Repay me for my loss. And yet I will
Accept the end results of Yahweh's plan;
Hurt though it will, Rebekah certainly,
As I have said, shall leave with you. And now,
My friends," he told his guests, "sit down and be
At last refreshed!" Then did Eli allow
Naught else to further keep them from the choice,
Delicious meal for which they'd yearned. So they
Sat down and feasted. Following Laban's voice
When they were done, through gloom they made their way
Out to their quarters quickly, that they might
Rest there for the remainder of the night.

Early the following morning, they awoke
And quietly arose. Soon, summoned by
Nahor's grandson, they came before the folk
Of Bethuel's household, whom now Eli
Addressed. "Bid me at once to head back to
The dwelling of my master," he implored
His hosts. "I must not linger here with you,
Though you've shown such great kindness to my lord."
"One daughter I, in all my many years,
Have borne," the mother of the girl then said.
"I ask you, please, be mindful of the tears
My eyes since last night ceaselessly have shed.
Can she not stay here for another week
Or two?" Then did the maiden's brother speak:

"Nine days after tomorrow: Would you be
Content to leave then, Eli?" "We today,"
Eli insisted, "ought to leave. Let me
Return to Abraham without delay,
Now that Yahweh has granted me success."
Inquired they of Rebekah, then, if she
Now wished to set out. And she answered, "Yes.
Go with this man today I will. To be
The girl betrothed to Isaac thrilled I am!
He will be my first lover—I deny
It not. In me the heir of Abraham
Shall take delight; and he shall satisfy
My thirst for love. Yes, we will leave today
And head for my new home without delay!"

"Thus shall it be," her father said. And so
The matter was decided. In that room,
Emotions now ran high as to and fro
Rebekah, radiant as a flower in bloom,
Trod briskly, making sure to fondly bid
Her family and their servants all farewell.
Eli's men at his word, however, did
Not linger in the house of Bethuel:
They, told for their departure to prepare,
Headed outside. But, rooted like a tree,
Eli moved not. "My sister, may you fare,"
Said Laban at one point, "most splendidly,
Evading misery and ruin. May
Rich, lavish blessings ever come your way!

"Violent, aggressive, weapon-wielding men
Against your clan might someday march: May your
Number increase to thousands, so that when
Those men declare on your descendants war,
The victors in each battle will be your
Offspring, who'll thus possess the gates of their
Opponents!" Silence filled the room once more.
Kindly yet firmly, having walked to where
The maiden and her mother now embraced,
Eli asked, "Have you packed?" The girl delayed
No more, but gathered up her things and raced
Outside with them. Her preparations made
For the long trip, she paused to rest beside
Her camel. At that moment, Eli cried:

"It's time!" The travellers then, without delay,
Set out from Nahor. Ere that day was done,
Much ground the company had covered. Day
After long day, warmed by the radiant sun,
Swiftly they journeyed. Upon being told
That the girl's nose had finally fully healed,
Eli, who'd pierced it with the ring of gold,
Rejoiced and praised Yahweh. Onto a field
Shrouded in shade one evening, as the sun
Crept down behind a distant hill, they came.
Across the open field they spied someone
Making his way towards them. His tall, broad frame
Eli knew well: "Behold, fair maiden: My
Lord's son—your one true love—" he cried, "draws nigh!"

VII: Isaac and Rebekah

Sky-high did Isaac's spirit soar:
As fair a story as his ears
Now heard, he'd never known; his fears
Dissolved that all his days he'd spend
Lacking the love he'd long yearned for.

Excited by the epic tale,
For hours fail to fall asleep
That night he did: The thrill, so deep,
That now consumed his thoughts, kept him
All night as restless as a gale.

Kind, gentle sunlight kissed the earth,
Inspiring mirth in Isaac's clan:
Night done now, day anew began.
Great was this day, whose glorious end
Witnessed joint vows of weight and worth.

Isaac, at dusk, took in his hand
The maiden's and swore then to love
Her as himself. Said he, "Times of
Hardship will come, when hope grows dim;
In ill times, by you I'll yet stand.

"My wife, till death parts me and you
At last, you'll truly always be."
"Last our love shall, as long as we
Live," said Rebekah, "—lest heartache,
Keen as a knife, we know anew."

In marriage, watched by Isaac's clan,
Now that good man, that noble heir,
Did join, as dusk grew deep, the fair,
Sweet, virtuous maiden. So their age
Of oneness all at once began.

Fulfillment then they found, with quite
Glad hearts, that night, good gifts to each
Other—formerly out of reach—
Offering: In each other take
Delight they did ere day's first light.

Together, now, those two Yahweh
Held fast; and they, their hearts' desire—
Intense—indeed, an infinite fire—
Now met, entered a new life-stage
Gladly that good and glorious day.

Part Two:

The Song of

Rebekah

Seasons have passed, year after year,
Forgetting that I am waiting for the
Rightful man to appear, to make me his bride.
Oh, to find that companionship would be
Miraculous, solely provided by God's gracious
Hands. And so I wait, attending to my daily duties.
In the waiting, ever faithfully for my companion
Shall I pray, preparing my heart for when
My groom and I will meet face to face.

As time presses on, I am overcome with an indelible
Sadness. Will I forever be alone, never to be
Taken by a man who will make me his wife?
Even lowly creatures have found and felt fondness,
Relieved to be seen, to be held, to be loved.
Here am I, a simple, lonely girl, earnestly and
Eagerly waiting to be seen by one man who, upon
Searching for his one true love, will
Eventually find his footsteps leading to me.

Tomorrow is a new day, and I will breathe again.
Only God, God alone, knows how each day will
Unfold. With my gaze toward my future, I'll arise.
Toward God, I will aim my heart and mind, so to
Find peace for the days of waiting, believing it
Over, will soon be. The God of Abraham
Respects my desires, and listens to what I
Ask. Appealing to Him, I will make known my
Request: A husband is what I yearn for most.

As dusk approaches, to the spring I must go.
My task — to draw water that will quench the thirsts of
Not only myself, but the family that raised me
And taught me to be gentle, gracious, generous, and
Hospitable to all who pass my way, to readily
Accommodate the needs of others with kindness,
Reflecting God. With this in my heart,
A stranger I saw approaching the well. Politely, he
Inquired if, from my jar, a drink he could receive.

My heart leapt at once for the opportunity to
Assist this man in need. As I let down my jar, he
Nimbly took a satisfying sip. I then tended to his camels,
Drawing water to refresh their parched mouths. As
My water jar was emptying, the man inquired of me,
Asking who I was and for a place to stay. "Bethuel's
Daughter am I," was my response, and his attentive
Eyes widened at my words. An invitation I gave to
Him and his men, a warm place to stay for the night.

In gratitude, the stranger bowed to worship God,
Speaking of success in his journey. For God had revealed
What direction he would need to take in order to
Arrive at his master's relatives' dwelling place.
Yet before bowing in admiration, though tired from the
Trek was he, the man, for my adornment,
Out of his pockets carefully and delightedly
Took two gold bracelets and a gleaming nose ring.
His prayers wonderfully answered, and mine, as well.

Ever so promptly, I withdrew from the well
To tell my mother of all that had taken place.
Out of our home Laban hurried along, making his
Way to the spring where the stranger had remained.
No delay was to be had as he, with friendliness,
Opened our abode to the men and gave straw to the camels.
Food was prepared, and the men washed their feet. But
No dining would occur until the stranger had a moment to
Articulate all the important details he had to share.

He introduced himself as Abraham's servant, and
Oh, what a wondrous revelation that was to hear!
Richly blessed had Abraham become, wealthy in
His olden age. A widower was he, with a son emptied of
Enthusiasm for life, mourning the passing of
His mother, resigning himself to believing that forever
Alone would he be — that no bride would be
Discovered, that he would live out his days
Troubled, downtrodden, with no hope for love.

His father, Abraham, knowing of his despair,
Employed his head servant, Eliezer, to leave their
City and travel to our land with the purpose of
Acquiring a wife for his destitute and lonely son.
Minutes passed as the servant continued expressing
Each important detail. Upon finishing his account,
Laban and my father proclaimed, "The Lord has
Spoken. Here is Rebekah, take her. She will be
Kin to Abraham, wife to your master's son."

Not much sleep did find me that night, as
Elation of my future grabbed ahold of my thoughts.
Early in the morning, I anxiously packed my belongings,
Letting my mind wander, wondering what the coming
Days would involve. A lengthy journey awaited me,
One that would lead to a future I had long prayed for.
Who was this man that would become my husband?
No details were revealed to me, only that Abraham's son
Now would also know love and answered prayers.

Even so, in my wonderings, hope had returned to my soul.
As we moved throughout the land, confidence and
Reassurance returned to my bones. I would know love, too.
The years of waiting, long though they were, were
Hastily coming to an end. My heart could care not how
Effortful the pilgrimage was, for my thoughts, focused,
Were on what would lie ahead — my future, bright and luminous.
Elated was I to arrive in Hebron. The journey of great
Length was over. My dreams were drawing nearer.

Long had I prayed for a man of integrity, a man
Of great character and faith. And as I looked
Up, across the field I saw a man that looked
To be meditating, praying to his Lord. What I
Saw, to be sure, was a man that seemed honest and good. Could
I, Rebekah, be looking at my groom? These thoughts
Did consume me, so I asked Eliezer who the man, now
Ever so attentive to my appearance, was. Without pause,
The servant answered, "That is my master, Isaac."

Hurriedly, I covered my face with my veil, although my
Excitement was growing quite fast. I knew in my heart
That Isaac was to be my companion, the single
One I had prayed for and waited for. But, then,
Why was I anxious? Why so afraid? For knowing
Not who Isaac truly was, I committed to grow closer to him.
Isaac and I became husband and wife, a bond
That would only be broken by death. Our hearts had
Waned long enough. Our love for each other we'd find.

A healing would come to my one love, my groom.
Such comfort I was glad to provide to Isaac, for
The death of his mother had weighed on him mightily.
Overcoming grief, overcoming anguish, finally
We could look forward to our future together.
Alone no more, we would worship as one. And I,
Rebekah, could finally be loved, for Isaac,
Devoted to me fully, would show me love
Evermore, since vowing himself to me in marriage.

Vast was the fog of sadness that in the past seemed to
Entrench my life, as daily I'd lived, lonely, with
No groom to love. And now, my life has changed, as
Isaac my hope renewed, and I his hope revived.
Nothing will separate our braided bond as we
Go together throughout our lives. God has
Truly answered our prayers, two lovers divided, now
Healing together — our woes leaving us, replaced only by
Excitement for a future that holds more hope than the past.

Time will persist, and each morning I'll rise with
Isaac by my side. A man committed to his faith in God, a
Man committed to loving me. I waited so long, like an
Eternity it felt. So for all of my days, I shall cherish
These moments, making memories and creating life as
Husband and wife, together. Seasons will pass,
Ebbing and flowing with what existence entails, and I
Will walk with my jar to the well to fetch water,
Openly grateful for the love I've received.

May my heart and my mind never forget the encounter with
Eliezer that day that changed my life for good.
New hope sprang up from the well that day,
Gifting me with a husband, a lover, with Isaac.
Over mountains and valleys Eliezer and his men set
Out to seek for Isaac a bride, and surely, though
Unbeknownst to anyone, that bride would be me,
The simple, lonely girl that prayed each day,
That hoped and longed for a love all my own.

Onward our lives will go, enriched by the love we
Draw from one another. My deep solitude has been
Relinquished, and Isaac has been, by God's grace,
Awakened from his dark mourning, made new
With delight as with me, his wife, he dwells.
What more could I ask for in this life I am living?
A yearning that emblazoned my heart has been fulfilled —
That I would find a groom, and that I could be a bride.
Each day I am thankful to love once more and be loved once more.

Rising up, to the well I will go to draw water for Isaac, my love.

Glossary

Archaic and rare words and their meanings:

descried—perceived (22, 36)

ere—before (5, 8, 13, 22, 26, 27, 30, 31, 32, 37, 45, 50, 53)

fare—get along in life (49)

fared—travelled (18)

feigned—pretended (8, 9)

hence—from here (38)

mirth—happiness (12, 52)

naught—nothing (14, 42, 47)

nigh—near (13, 22, 27, 28, 31, 34, 39, 43, 50)

o'er—over (8, 12, 18, 26, 46)

sundered—separated (47)

visage—face (26)

troth—promise (19)

whence—from where (26, 37)

www.ingramcontent.com/pod-product-compliance
Lightning Source LLC
Chambersburg PA
CBHW020335130626
46549CB00003B/1182